How to be a great
GOAT

First published 2024

Copyright © Ian Phillips 2024

The right of Ian Phillips to be identified as the author of this work has been asserted in accordance with the Copyright, Designs & Patents Act 1988.

All rights reserved. No part of this book may be reproduced, stored in a retrieval system, or transmitted in any form or by any means, digital, electronic, electrostatic, magnetic tape, mechanical, photocopying, recording or otherwise, without the written permission of the copyright holder.

Published under licence by Brown Dog Books and
The Self-Publishing Partnership Ltd, 10b Greenway Farm, Bath Rd, Wick, nr. Bath BS30 5RL, UK

www.selfpublishingpartnership.co.uk

ISBN printed book: 978-1-83952-791-3
ISBN e-book: 978-1-83952-792-0

Cover design by Kevin Rylands
Internal design by Andrew Easton

Printed and bound in the UK

This book is printed on FSC® certified paper

How to be a great
GoaT

*A guide to being a brilliant
Governor or a Trustee*

IAN PHILLIPS

Foreword by Emma Balchin, Co-Chief Executive
National Governance Association

Contents

Foreword	7
Introduction	9
The Attributes of Great GoaTs	11
Independence	12
Challenge	14
Listening	17
Support	19
Curiosity	21
Humility	23
Conscientiousness	25
Pessimism	28
Intolerance	31
Resilience	33
Self-improvement	37
Self-criticism	41
The Scope of GoaTship	43
Strategy	44
Finance	48
Performance Management	52
Risk	59
Succession Planning	61

Crisis resolution	65
The Chief GoaT	68
The art of chairing	69
The Tribe of GoaTs	74
Hallmarks of Excellence	75
The Clerk	80
A Particular Breed of GoaT	83
Members: the Overseers' Overseers	84
Nolan	88
Best Behaviour	89
A Stimulus to Challenge	91
No-Conflict Questions	92
And, finally, Exiting your GoaTship	94
Avoiding the Dread	95
Some Case Studies and Tools	98
Governance charter model	99
Academy crisis resolution case study	100
School transformation case study	101
Leader recruitment flowchart	102
Skills audit + board profile model	103
Model Pros & Cons 1-pager	104
Model Project Investment Proposal	105
About the Author	106
A Timeline in Education & Governance	107
About the Sponsor	108
Notes	110

Foreword

A quarter of a million people in England volunteer to govern state schools and academy trusts, and if you are reading this book, it is likely that you are one of them. Now, more than ever, schools and their leaders need the support of committed individuals who are also willing to hold them to account on behalf of their pupils.

At the National Governance Association (NGA) we are privileged to support and represent governors and trustees, and the governance professionals who serve their boards. We welcome this contribution to the growing body of information, advice and guidance available to governors and trustees, or, as this book fondly refers to them, GoaTs!

Most books about governance focus on process. This personal memoir detailing the experiences of two decades governing, seeks more to help governors and trustees to understand the nature of the role with a welcomed focus on effective behaviours and culture. Often chairing schools with significant strategic challenges, Ian Phillips has distilled his experiences into a series of attributes shared by effective governors, trustees, chairs, and trust members – and the consequences of not exhibiting these characteristics.

FOREWORD

If you have a story to tell or questions to ask after reading this book, please do get in touch. We aim to make visible the crucial work governing boards do to ensure children and young people get the best possible education. Please join us in our efforts to further raise the profile of the role, celebrating the successes, and sharing the lessons learned so others may learn and grow from them.

Thank you, as always, for your hard work. We hope that in reading this book many GoaTs take up the invitation (and challenge) to be as great as they can be.

Emma Balchin
Co-Chief Executive, National Governance Association

Introduction

'Be not afraid of greatness: some are born great, some achieve greatness, and some have greatness thrust upon them.'
William Shakespeare

GoaT is part-guide, part-memoir. Its purpose is simple – to help GoaTs be as great as they can be.

First things first, what's a GoaT? It's this book's shorthand for a Governor or a Trustee.

Because the insights in here apply equally to a school or college governor, or a trustee within an academy.

The ideas, habits and attitudes apply regardless of the constitution of an educational establishment. And some of the less successful behaviours are – shall we say – indiscriminate in their choice of arena.

The motivation behind *GoaT* is to share various experiences from two decades as a chair, governor, trustee, trust member and National Leader of Governance. Every example given is drawn from personal experience.

The objective is to help colleagues right across the education landscape to be the best GoaTs that they can be. And thereby enjoy a rich and rewarding experience, while adding real value

INTRODUCTION

to our schools and colleges.

I hope it is welcomed by that great tribe of GoaTs which performs its noble, and largely unsung, work across Early Years, all Key Stages and beyond.

This book is testament to the many friends and colleagues I've met around the board table. It wouldn't exist without them. Needless to say, all opinions are entirely my own.

None of us could do what we do without the support of our partners who put up stoically with the many calls on our time. So, above all, *GoaT* is a tribute to mine, the wonderful Elaine.

Ian Phillips
Spring 2024

The Attributes of Great GoaTs

What it takes to be a great GoaT

Independence

'Man is born free and everywhere he is in chains.'
Jean-Jacques Rousseau

GoaTs are special people, putting themselves forward to serve willingly.

They join a community, yet must cling fiercely to their individuality.

There is no greater danger to effective governance than GoaTs who lose the feel of who they are, and why they're at the table.

This happens most particularly when there is misplaced sense of allegiance or gratitude to a school leader or the person who facilitated the opportunity to serve.

So, for example, a Trust board with at least 50 per cent of its trustees closely connected to the Head abdicated its sense of purpose and approved building projects that exhausted the school's reserves plus a large slice of the in-year budget. And with no business plan to show how either the money was being spent or would pay for itself.

GoaTs should not chain themselves to factions or individuals. Even those who are appointed as parents, students or even trust sponsors, owe their loyalty only to the school, college or (in the case of a multi-academy trust) the trust itself.

They represent no-one but themselves, bringing their values, know-how, knowledge and experience to bear on a board's deliberations and decision-making.

Boards are not forums for advocacy, but for the independent and free exchange of ideas, opinions and perspectives.

Even those who hold strong political or religious views should leave them outside the door so they can operate independently of them, using only what is in the best interests of the school as their compass.

And the best way to maintain independence?

Keep hold of these golden threads of governance:

Always act in the best interests of learners and staff

GoaTs employ leaders, and not the other way round

All GoaTs are equal

Never compromise excellence for expedience

Ask questions, even if you're the only one

Feel free to push back, even after the meeting

Don't wait until the meeting to clarify any documents.

Challenge

'I beseech you … think it possible you may be mistaken.'
Oliver Cromwell

This is the most important function of GoaTs. And the one that can be the most discomfiting. There is no sin greater than being supine.

Some GoaTs remember their time at school, and find it unnerving to take issue with headteachers. And parent and student GoaTs may be reluctant to stand up to a key authority figure in their lives.

What does challenge look like in a well-functioning board?

First of all, it's polite and respectful. There are GoaTs who think that their job is to butt heads (sorry) with those in leadership positions. It isn't.

Challenge is about asking constructive questions.

Why this approach?

૭

What do peer organisations do?

૭

Have we always done it this way?

Why now?

What other ways have you considered to deal with this?

The purpose is to find better ways of doing things. Or, at least, to be reassured that the chosen path is the best available. That is why GoaTs are sat round the table – to optimise the chances of getting things right as often as possible.

Witness the experienced board of a financially outstanding college when it received a somewhat scanty business proposal to install solar panels on the roof of a building.

First, they asked: *What's the payback?*

And then: *Is there not something we can spend the money on of more direct benefit to students?*

This was not initially well received by the leadership. After all, this was the way it had always been done – and the college was strong on all fronts.

But 'If it ain't broke, don't fix it' must acknowledge its essential impotence as it gives ground to the quest for perpetual improvement.

The result? A formal approach to capital investment that ensured simple, comprehensive business cases as a precursor to decision-making. You can find the model on page 105.

And then there's the opposite. What if we don't challenge? That's not a licence to take issue with everything. But it is an invitation to consider the likely outcomes if uncomfortable issues are invariably avoided.

If leaders feel they won't be held to account, there is a real risk of a culture of complacency infecting leadership. A must to prevent.

Listening

'Wisdom is the reward you get for a lifetime of listening when you would have rather talked.'
Mark Twain

Being a GoaT involves a lot of listening.

One of the great benefits of service on an education board is that its collegiate atmosphere allows you to hone your listening skills.

Among the more rewarding aspects of educational governance is meeting strangers. Engaging with those who you would otherwise be unlikely to encounter broadens the mind and expands experience.

Generally, a student wouldn't expect to sit across the table from a chartered accountant or corporate lawyer.

A chemistry teacher would not imagine that their career would lead to entrepreneurs or speechwriters becoming colleagues.

Nor would someone dedicated to safeguarding children have thought that one day they would share decision-making responsibilities with an architect or a pastor.

And all, of course, vice-versa.

In the boardroom all voices are equal. And they have to be listened to with equal respect, even if a particular GoaT can be annoying.

So, here is just a handful of suggestions of how listening works on an effective board.

Every GoaT should try and focus on who is talking, weighing what they're saying and testing it against their own views and thoughts.

Even when one is eager to speak, it makes for effective dialogue if they give others the space to express their opinion.

Waiting one's turn while catching the Chair's eye (and remembering your point) adds to the sense of ordered debate.

Listening is, perhaps, the most important pre-requisite to embedded decision-making, especially where that decision is essential to the future of the organisation.

When something comes to the table, such as when a single academy trust had to decide whether to fold itself into a multi-academy trust, it's critical that all opinions are heard respectfully.

This kind of decision, from which there can be no rowing back, must be taken by everyone around the table in full knowledge of its irreversibility.

Listening – really *listening* – is the key both to consensus and a genuine understanding of all the implications of major issues and decisions.

Support

'The best way to find yourself is to lose yourself in the service of others.'
Mahatma Gandhi

Ask most GoaTs why they do it and the answer will most likely fall broadly under this heading.

Some will express it as 'giving something back'. Others as something like 'balancing the day job'. Still more will talk about 'joining a community'.

But motivations are, in truth, less relevant than the quality of service.

'Support' comes in several forms around the board table.

At its most basic, it is embracing the ethos of the school or college. This doesn't mean total immersion in the organisation. Distance lends objectivity, an essential attribute of effective governance.

GoaTs should try to go on learning walks to see teaching and learning in operation, while gaining a sense of how the ethos is being applied day in, day out. Showing one's face is an important part of evidencing support.

As is sharing experience and expertise. Every GoaT has

something to offer, whatever their background. Accepting a seat at the table means also accepting the obligation to contribute, each according to their personal know-how and knowledge.

A strong board is greater than the sum of its parts. Each member participates to the best of their abilities and, in doing so, strengthens the entire structure. It is a self-reliant, mutually supporting system that retains its structural integrity only for as long as everyone commits.

But let's also ponder what being supportive is NOT.

It's not nodding through decisions, just because they are proposed by the leadership.

It's not adopting the line of least resistance.

It's not skimming documents and trying to wing it during meetings.

It's not seeking allies or developing cliques.

It's not eye-rolling at colleagues when they go on a bit or drift off topic.

And it's most certainly not staying silent when challenging matters are discussed or difficult decisions required.

Curiosity

'The important thing is not to stop questioning. Curiosity has its own reason for existence.'
Albert Einstein

Effective GoaTs are self-feeders. They are hungry for knowledge, and greedy to understand how schools and colleges work.

Asking questions. Seeking explanations. Probing the reasons behind practices, decisions and behaviours. Without these, GoaTs are at best short-sighted, at worst wilfully blind.

Some are nervous about asking a question, fearing perhaps that they might seem ignorant or be missing the obvious. There is only one scenario where this is so – when the answer lies in papers presented to the board in advance of the meeting ... and they haven't been read beforehand.

Otherwise, a GoaT can't do the job if they don't feel able to ask questions. Observe the idiocy of one such beast. After four years serving on a Finance & Operations Committee, at his very last meeting, he admitted never to have understood the finances!

Imagine how things might have been different – how much richer and more rewarding his experience and contribution could have been – had he just said something at the outset.

Because the curious GoaT can be trained, mentored, buddied up, their learning curve shortened. But the incurious, the complacent, the downright arrogant can't.

So, be honest. Say 'I don't get it.' Demand that the technical terms be explained. Never pretend to know or to understand. No ambitious board or senior leadership team should resent an admission of ignorance if made with the hunger to improve. And, if they do, move on. They need you more than you do them, particularly as they don't know it. Yet.

Humility

'I am still learning.'
Michelangelo

If one of the transcendental geniuses can have as his motto the explicit ambition to continue learning, then who are we mere mortals to set our bar lower?

When GoaTs come to the table for the first time, they bring with them the accumulated experiences of their life to that point. And their presence is an unambiguous commitment both to contribute, and to learn.

But they need to do so while recognising that they don't know everything.

Humility is a two-way street. It's not just about acknowledging the need to self-improve. It also means that not every skill is transferable unamended into an educational setting.

One of the frustrations that those from the business world can find when joining schools and colleges is that decision-making can be laboured, and project timescales protracted.

At times like this, when the temptation to display impatience may seem irresistible, take a breath. Great GoaTs recognise that they are travelling a different landscape, and that it is they who must find a way of sustaining themselves when there.

It's not constructive to take an adversarial stance if, for example, data appears contradictory or inconsistent. Rather, say 'I'm struggling to understand this. Can we discuss it offline?'

And the key signs of humility?

A board and members that regularly seek self-improvement and accept the need for training.

Second, one that systematically reviews its skills and identifies what are lacking or may be needed in the future. There's a model skills audit (and demographic breakdown of boards) on page 103.

And third, where the Chair has the honesty to recognise that a particular GoaT isn't working out and needs to be moved on.

Conscientiousness

'Our duty is to be useful, not according to our desires but according to our powers.'
Henri-Frédéric Amiel

What does a truly conscientious GoaT look like?

It's someone who masters what could be called the 'work:work balance'.

Being a GoaT is a job, not a hobby. And it often entails some friction with the dominant parts of people's lives.

Taking on the role means triangulating the three cornerstones of effective governance:

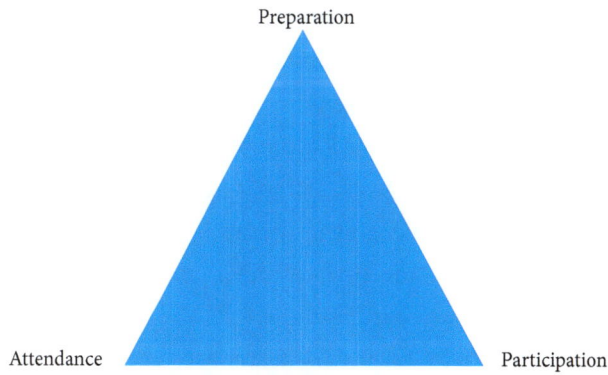

If any one of these is missing, then the whole structure is undermined.

To attend without preparation or participation is futile and hogs a place at the table that might otherwise be occupied by someone able to invest both time and effort.

To prepare and not attend precludes participation and essentially squanders the energy invested in that preparation.

To attend and participate without preparation is a GoaT's cardinal sin. Not only is it a waste of their time, but also colleagues'.

It is among the more exasperating aspects of being a GoaT when a fellow board member asks questions already dealt with in the pre-meeting pack, or feels able (invariably wrongly) to wing it.

Imagine the feelings of a National Leader of Governance asked to review performance and seeing the majority of governors switch off during the item on finance, a good number of them actually looking at their mobiles.

Or the candidate for Chair who appeared never to have considered either the role description or workload before throwing their hat in the ring.

So, the conscientious GoaT is one who immerses themselves in the pre-meeting pack, preparing questions, seeking explanations, and challenging proposals.

They arrive at a meeting, whether real or virtual, fully prepared and ready to participate.

Of course, sometimes events intervene to prevent attendance. This is always understandable. Everyone recognises that life outside can interfere. Many GoaTs have demanding jobs, while staff, parents and students inevitably have to fit their obligations into crowded personal schedules.

Some slack will always have to be cut, but the truly self-aware and self-critical GoaT knows when they're not pulling their weight. Together with the Chair they find a way of improving the situation or, reluctantly, call it a day.

Pessimism

'Ah! Oh, don't the days seem lank and long
When all goes right and nothing goes wrong,
And isn't your life extremely flat
With nothing whatever to grumble at.'
WS Gilbert

A quick maxim (with no philosophical or moral foundation whatsoever): Leaders should be optimistic; GoaTs not so much.

It is for Heads, Principals and Chief Execs to come to the board with proposals concerning the improvement of the school, college or trust.

And it's for GoaTs to stand back and ask: 'Ok, sounds great. Now, what can go wrong?'

Those who come from a business background in particular should bear this in mind: most educational leaders are professional teachers who have morphed into directors of social enterprises.

They will not necessarily be versed in analytical techniques like sensitivity analyses, project stress-testing or even forensic SWOT (Strengths, Weaknesses, Opportunities, Threats) and PEST (Political, Economic, Social, Technological) evaluations.

And, while risk management should be at the heart of annual planning, it is less likely to form part of a business proposal.

So, the challenge for GoaTs is to identify the soft underbelly of propositions, balancing all the time so as to be supportive, not negative.

It is one of the more annoying human traits that people end up advocating for ideas and take it personally if they are questioned.

A well-chaired board will avoid that and ensure that GoaTs' pessimism is part of the common wealth of the community. After all, no-one seeks failure or underperformance.

Pessimism can be a sharp scalpel to peel back the layers of a proposal. We saw earlier where a business case for solar panels was anything but robust.

But see what happened when a degree of naivety collided with a phalanx of pessimists. The plan was to spend a six-figure sum refurbishing and repairing a stand-alone building.

Governors were on board until a bomb dropped. Leaders had discovered that the location within a wholly-owned site was actually held by the local authority under a long-forgotten 125-year lease.

In other words – to the astonishment of all – the building wasn't actually controlled by the organisation.

After jaws had been lifted from table, pessimism ran riot. This particular flock of GoaTs included a lawyer, an accountant and two experienced businesspeople.

Once the leadership had accepted some pretty dire consequences of progressing the proposal, the bleak prognosis gave way rapidly to a new course of action: get back the title to the property so that leaders once more had control over the entire site.

Eventually (after over three years), tenacity and patience won out, and the corporation could, once more, exercise full ownership over the whole site.

Intolerance

'Mediocrity knows nothing higher than itself, but talent instantly recognises genius.'
Sir Arthur Conan Doyle

It may seem strange in this era of equality and diversity to promote intolerance as an attribute of great governance.

But, hopefully, this section's quotation gives the game away.

GoaTs must be totally intolerant of mediocrity. Indeed, they should regard excellence as the absolute norm.

For many, an understanding of what that looks like can be elusive. So let's try illustration, rather than definition.

A single academy trust board had signed off its annual accounts. They were littered with typographical errors, some of them perpetuated year after year after year.

It raised some questions about trustees' attitudes and respect for detail (apart from the reliability of the auditors).

Had successive trustees not read them before approval?

Or: Had trustees read them but only superficially, with zero critical filters or ignorance of basic spelling and grammar?

Or: Had trustees read them, seen the errors – but didn't care enough to block approval?

Each reader can decide for themselves which of these is worse.

On the other side of the coin, see how the boards of two schools who were amalgamating responded to the need to review every policy of the emergent school.

Among an atypically large bundle for the last meeting before formal merger, they read eight detailed policies. Every member questioned how the Heads of the two schools had arrived at their content when their individual versions had diverged. Not only that, governors had also identified many errors, typographical and otherwise.

Only by a concentrated and forensic reading can such things be achieved.

There are no short cuts. Great GoaTs on great boards recognise that, and put in the work to achieve zero tolerance of mediocrity or complacency.

Resilience

'The greatest glory in living lies not in never falling, but in rising every time we fall.'
Nelson Mandela

Most GoaTs embark upon their governance journey in blissful ignorance of all the potential pitfalls that may beset a school or college.

During the recruitment stage, they will learn about the institution and be inducted into the role, hopefully in tandem with a role description of some sort.

But, as any GoaT who has been in post when a crisis hits knows, there is little preparation that can be done, either to prevent it or even be ready for it. (This is different from risk management, which we'll deal with soon.)

And so one measure of GoaT greatness is how they rise to the challenge … and what kind of organisation emerges once the dust has settled.

Here, there could be a marked difference, depending on foundation status.

MATs and SATs will have varying levels of governance and leadership heft to deploy both in resolving a crisis and repairing whatever it damaged.

SATs, in particular, may need to source external support as a matter of urgency.

The capacity for community schools to respond and withstand a crisis will depend on the level of their local authority's readiness to be proactive. In any event, the LEA will almost certainly drive the resolution.

Resilience can be tested in any number of ways. A school that Ofsted downgrades to 'requires improvement' or 'inadequate' is immediately plunged into fervent introspection (at best) or complete meltdown.

Identifying the root causes of this failure – and setting out the path to rectify them – will be long-term … and painful. It is unlikely all those in post pre-inspection will remain so.

If a financial scandal is revealed, then it will fall to GoaTs to assume more hands-on leadership in order to get to the bottom both of responsibility and impact. If institutional leaders have been negligent, duped or, worst of all, complicit, this will trigger existential angst that may well be resolved by external authorities, like the Education and Skills Funding Agency (ESFA).

It's at times like this that GoaTs must keep a level head – and ask themselves, as individuals and as a collective – the hard questions.

How could we have let this happen?

How might we have prevented it?

What systems and processes must we install to ensure stability and resilience?

RESILIENCE

Once answered honestly, the ways in which the board and the organisation bounce back will be how the community entrusted to them will remember their service.

So, put yourself in the shoes of a GoaT at a two-school, faith-based MAT.

A student had been permanently excluded. As per its policy, a panel of trustees and local governors was convened. It listened to both sides and decided that the exclusion should be ratified.

The panel then came under significant pressure from the wider community to reverse its decision. And did so.

Cue chaos, with the student left in limbo on an extended absence. The trust sought legal advice, and both the original decision and its subsequent reversal were nullified.

Moreover, it was clear that a robust panel could not be resourced from within. Lawyers determined that a new, effectively single-purpose sub-committee be arranged made up entirely of external volunteers.

Its decision after a six-hour hearing with the student represented by counsel and the school not? Reinstatement, as there had been a clear failure to follow the statutory guidance.

The outcome raised some pretty profound questions of governance that all GoaTs across the trust should have been asking.

How could the trust not populate an effective and reliable panel from within its own family?

Why did the first panel support the original decision when external, highly-experienced outsiders overturned it?

What does this episode tell us about the quality of leadership, both in the school and across the wider trust?

Are our own GoaTs really up to the job?

How could we benefit from external advice, guidance and support to raise our governance game?

The external panel certainly formed the view that governance was seriously lacking and even debated what, if anything, they should do about it.

Now ask yourself: What would *I* have done if I'd been a GoaT there?

A key component of resilience is recognising the need to be resilient, acknowledging the issue from which recovery is required.

And, uncomfortable though it is, a GoaT must sometimes stand up, even if they are on their own. As Gandhi said: 'Even if you are a minority of one, the truth is the truth.'

Self-improvement

'Public service is a stimulating, proud and lively enterprise. It is not just a way of life, it is a way to live fully.'
Lee H Hamilton

Being a GoaT is a journey. Most start it knowing very little.
It may be the first time you've sat around a board table. Or gone into a school since you or your own kids were in education.

You may be an entrepreneur, master/mistress of all you survey, and now part of a collegiate community where all are equals.

On the other hand, you could be a parent or carer wishing to participate in decision-making that will affect your child's future.

Whatever the path that brought you to the boardroom, you should know one thing.

You have willingly agreed to expand your knowledge, skills and experience to meet the demands of the job and the needs of the organisation.

This will mean submitting yourself to a number of disciplines that may be unfamiliar.

Like many (all?) sectors, education has its own vocabulary, one reasonably described as a FoA (Forest of Acronyms).

And it frequently happens that the professionals in the room won't always recall that most GoaTs are outsiders.

So much so, that some schools and colleges actually produce a glossary of terms and abbreviations.

Part of the self-improvement journey is to master the most used terms, whether that's in presentations or on the various spreadsheets where abbreviations are the norm.

But there's much more to it than memorising technical words and phrases.

GoaTs are on a permanent learning curve. Life in education is constantly changing and invariably full of surprises.

Some can be prepared for by formal coaching. Others require a more instinctive response.

Take safeguarding, for example.

Every year there should be training, both to update and remind.

But, in truth, proving that boards can demonstrate in-depth safeguarding knowledge is different from active governance.

That comes when a real crisis hits.

The older the learners, the fewer the incidents. But what they lack in frequency, they gain in gravity. Safeguarding events in primary settings are far more common but not generally too severe.

Sixth form students are a different beast altogether. In the main, they are committed and passionate. So, when something happens that triggers a safeguarding alert, boards should expect something serious. Of course, GoaTs will reach for the policy, guided by the institution's Designated Safeguarding Lead and the board's nominated GoaT. But that's just the start.

How GoaTs support the leadership at sensitive times is a key indicator of excellence.

Few schools and colleges have crisis management plans. When an incident hits, there aren't always protocols to roll out.

This is when boards learn 'on the job'.

Immediate briefings on the nature of the event, and its possible repercussions. The institution's response. And, perhaps most importantly, the reputational and other risks that follow in its wake.

All these make for a near-vertical high-board plunge into the world of damage limitation.

And the challenge needs to be embraced enthusiastically, both for the immediate good of the school, and for the collective learning that becomes embedded into the intellectual capital of the board and its GoaTs.

It's the same with Ofsted.

All GoaTs should be on top of what will be expected when the inspectors call.

Annual training and refreshers help to keep the inevitability of an inspection in front of mind, particularly where the next due date begins to dawn.

The purpose of this is to help those who meet Ofsted to be ready for what they may be asked.

As notice is always short, availability may mean that anyone might be needed.

There's no way to be certain that all GoaTs are prepared. The best that can be hoped for is that those who meet inspectors are confident in their knowledge and understanding of how the organisation works as a learning environment.

At the time of writing, the future of Ofsted is looking distinctly uncertain. A new Chief Inspector, a Labour Party already committed to reform if it wins power – and an inquest hovering over the organisation like the sword of Damocles.

We may even be at the dawn of an enlightened inspection regime that no longer strikes fear in the hearts of schools – and their GoaTs. One can only hope.

Self-criticism

'I'm beginning to notice some improvement.'
Pablo Casals

When Casals thus answered the question of why he continued to practise three hours a day aged ninety-three, the world's greatest-ever cellist captured an essential truth.

Those aspiring to be great GoaTs never rest on their laurels. Even after stellar results or an Outstanding Ofsted, they ask:

What could be done even better?

୨

How do we avoid complacency?

୨

What can we learn from other exceptional providers?

But there's more.

How can I as an individual GoaT have done better?

୨

Was I always as prepared as I should have been?

Did I contribute to the best of my abilities?

Were there meetings when I was disengaged?

And so on.

This introspection is not confined to singular GoaTs. The whole board should be assessing its performance, annually against a rigorous scorecard-based self-assessment.

What's more, boards with a hunger to be as great as they can be should subject themselves to a periodic external review of governance.

Only in this way can all those involved have confidence that what they're actually doing is both effective and tracking best-in-class performance.

Objectivity is key here. A sixth form college which (incorrectly) trusted Ofsted that its governance was 'Good' invited a National Leader of Governance to identify areas that, with improvement, could lead to it being 'Outstanding'.

After a thorough review, the NLG determined that, as far as governance was concerned, the college 'required improvement'.

It may not be a coincidence that, the year after, Ofsted mirrored that opinion in its overall judgement.

The college is no longer independent, but part of a larger group.

Perhaps if they had implemented the recommendations, it would have made a difference. We will never know.

The Scope of GoaTship

Now let's look at how these attributes work across some of the principal areas of a GoaT's work.

Strategy

'The biggest risk is not taking any risk. In a world that's changing really quickly, the only strategy that is guaranteed to fail is not taking risks.'
Mark Zuckerberg

Of the three main areas for GoaTs to concentrate on – strategy, performance management and finance – the first has the greatest potential for fractious debate and protracted decision-making.

In the days before academies and free schools, most boards did not have to concern themselves too much with strategy.

They could focus on specific issues, like outcomes and budgets, without having to ponder the future, with all its attendant risks and rewards.

So, how should GoaTs rise to this fundamental challenge?

The short answer: with an open mind. And with one question burning itself on the whole board: what's in the best interests of learners?

When GoaTs gather around the table, there will be a wide disparity in the appetite – or even the need – for risk-taking.

This is one of the areas of governance where people can

STRATEGY

fall prey to 'my-idea-itis' or, worse still, 'Plumber's Tut'.[1] Securing objective and free-flowing debate requires impartial inputs and inclusive facilitation, in certain situations better done by a complete outsider.

One example of a balanced contribution: a SAT that was considering joining a MAT prepared for trustees, staff and unions a single-page capture of the pros and cons. It reduced the choice between staying as is or changing into a simple for and against for each option. (You can find an anonymised model of this approach on page 104.)

As well as simplifying understanding and explaining decisions, this approach worked well to remove any suggestion of advocacy for a particular outcome. This proved a powerful way of eliminating emotion and personalities from the equation.

And the more profound the issue, the greater the need for cold-eyed objectivity.

Here's one more. Two schools – one infants, the other juniors. They share a site and a name, but one is community, the other foundation.

The boards of both schools were facing the same challenges – falling rolls, with a planned reduction from three-form entry to two caused by a mixture of increased competition and changing demographics. These were amplified by poor outcomes for pupils, and uninviting buildings.

Neither school as a separate entity was viable, nor attractive

---

[1] To be practised before meetings in front of a mirror and consisting of synchronised slow, sad head-shaking, in-breathing through teeth, and a loud tutting.

to a MAT or federation.

So both sets of governors agreed that merger followed by de-duplication of roles was the only way to achieve sustainable stability.

They also recognised that they needed external help to make the union a reality, and a neutral Chair to reinforce the merger as one of equals.

The success of the process was ensured by governors having the vision to see a solution and the humility to recognise they couldn't realise it without specific support.

This was complemented by a collegiate culture both within each board and across the combined team. No voice drowned out others as they moved through all the available options before settling on amalgamation. (There's a flowchart case study of this transformation on page 101.)

But no two institutions are identical, so the key for GoaTs is to agree the overarching objectives at the outset, review all the available options, possibly with external support, and secure sign-off on the preferred route before progressing.

It takes strong chairing and a collective will to set the organisation on the right path to a secure future.

In the current climate, no school or college can afford not to consider the future. So here are some general questions GoaTs should be posing to themselves and to leaders:

Is our current operational model sustainable?

Does government policy threaten our current model, regardless of performance?

☙

Can we (continue to) thrive as a community school?

☙

Do financial projections threaten our security?

☙

When we review our SWOT, are we best placed to seize our opportunities and/or avoid the threats?

☙

Does our SLT possess the skill-set and bandwidth to enact the necessary deep-dive into options?

☙

Is our herd of GoaTs sufficiently skilled to shape and help implement strategic realignment?

☙

If not now, when?

Finance

'Rule No. 1: Never lose money.
Rule No. 2: Never forget Rule No. 1.'
Warren Buffett

… is the first mantra that every GoaT should recite three times before every meeting …

… even those who are uncomfortable when the talk comes round to finance. (And, yes, it's fair to assume that Warren Buffett never sat on the board of a state-funded school.)

The second mantra is: It's not the numbers themselves; it's about what they mean.

While the financial heavy lifting is usually done by a specialist committee, all GoaTs should understand the nuts-and-bolts financial position of the organisation – and what it suggests the future might look like.

Particularly – though by no means exclusively – where boards have a number of parent and staff representatives, simplification is key.

It is perhaps in this area, more than any other, that GoaTs can switch off. Finance data are always presented on spreadsheets.

Laypeople can find these both impenetrable and daunting, not to mention rather boring.

It is not infrequent that some lose focus, especially when discussions become really granular. And there is a particular danger of qualified GoaTs drifting from the open sea of oversight towards the rocks of management.

There is a tendency for leaders to present just too much information. For some, it's done with the noble intention of ensuring total transparency. But for others, it can be a technique to diminish scrutiny. Less is more. But more is less.

And seeing a document with every single line of expenditure itemised across a number of columns is pure overkill.

It's at times like this when GoaTs have to stand up and say exactly what they need to assure themselves of the organisation's financial realities … and their strategic significance.

Yes, they can rely on their colleagues who are financially qualified to read what the balance sheet and profit-and-loss account say. But every GoaT should understand where the finances stand, shorn of all technical speak and acronyms.

One simple way of achieving this is to ask for a one-page cover sheet to the management accounts that sets out the core data in tabular and graphic formats.

This kind of approach enables all GoaTs, regardless of their level of understanding, to grasp the essentials of the organisation's finances.

The key question is: What does the board need to know in order to assess the short-term financial outcomes, and the long-term prospects?

THE SCOPE OF GOATSHIP

With the former, it's vital that the implications of an imminent deficit are fully understood at the earliest opportunity. This could require significant cost-cutting and even staffing reductions. GoaTs need to steel themselves for some tough decisions (the like of which they never signed up for).

However, with the latter, those prospects flow naturally into wider, and more fundamental, discussions.

Take the case of a school that has, through controlled expansion, prudent management and effective income generation, built a robust reserve fund. And let us further imagine that its capacity to generate more income by growing the roll is strictly limited by the size of its site and the number of its facilities.

What is it to do when inflation eats away at its safety net and threatens a deficit within, say, five years?

GoaTs don't need to know the intricacies of accounting in order to participate in a strategic debate on how to avoid such an eventuality.

But they must know that such an outcome is possible. Then they can weigh up the risks, and formulate options.

But this can only be done when accessible information rips away the curtain of mystique which, all too often, is allowed to obscure the harsh realities of educational finance.

One more thing. The fact that other schools are already in – or contemplating – deficit is no reason for ignoring our own. There is a risk of a form of moral hazard where GoaTs (albeit, perhaps, unspoken) settle into a mindset that says *'It's up to the LEA or MAT to sort this, not us. If they want a school of this size in this place, then there is a price to pay. Our costs will always be higher than our income.'*

This line of thinking should never be a barrier to reviewing costs, staffing levels or foundation structure – if only to reassure ourselves that we have made the right choices.

Performance Management

'You cannot run away from a weakness; you must sometimes fight it out or perish. And if that be so, why not now, and where you stand?'
Robert Louis Stevenson

'Performance Management' is one of those terms that covers a variety of aspects which are critical to great governance.

So, let's unpack it.

Most important and prominent is the performance of learners. Somewhat like Finance, this is an area that is expressed in blizzards of data, much of it using abbreviation.

And it is also important to know that what the letters stand for is only one step towards understanding, first, what they mean and, then, what the trends signify.

So, in a school data report for, say, an infant school, pupil performance in reading, writing and maths will be measured against several criteria:

- WT: Working Towards (where they should be)
- WA: Working At (where they should be)
- GD: Greater Depth (working above age-related expectations)

- PKS: Pre-Key Stage: Working below the Key Stage 1 National Curriculum.

When presented with these types of data, GoaTs must interrogate them to ensure that directions of progress are in the right direction.

Not only that, they must seek meaningful comparisons. What does this mean?

For starters, it demands comparators with institutions that have similar cohorts. An exclusively academic sixth form's A-level results or Russell Group entrants should be set against like-minded schools and colleges not, say, a college that offers a majority of vocational qualifications alongside a smattering of academic subjects.

And GoaTs in primary education should be wary of looking at national data when their school has a high percentage of pupils with English as an Additional Language, or a significant cohort that meets disadvantage criteria. If they don't, they are effectively comparing their pupils' performance with rural schools that have low (or even no) EAL learners, or those in areas of relative affluence.

There's no point to this. GoaTs invariably have finite time to give to their school or college. It's important that their investment is optimised.

So, in partnership with the leadership team, they should agree the key measures of performance – and interrogate them, if not mercilessly, then certainly robustly … and not accept fudges.

Here's an example of how this works in practice. A-levels have two measures: grades, and value-added. The second is intended as a gauge of how students have progressed in the two years since GCSEs.

A highly successful sixth form college noticed that its value-added dipped slightly into the red (i.e. students made negative progress).

Governors asked: Is it a blip or a trend?

The reply? We don't know, but will find out.

The following year it was markedly worse.

Governors: If it's not resolved, there will have to be changes. Please sort it out.

The next year, the measure was back in the black. Governors' firmness based on the data had driven a root-and-branch investigation. It revealed that in-bound students had, in the words of one teacher, not so much been spoon-fed to get their GCSE scores, as breast-fed.

Levels of independent learning were not high enough, and so Key Stage 4 results could not be relied upon as an accurate barometer of students' ability to meet the more exacting demands of Key Stage 5.

Cue faster, earlier induction into A-levels and more stringent in-year progress testing, alongside speedier support for those who were struggling.

The result? Sustainably positive value-added, even if some subjects were more volatile than others.

The overarching point here is, as Robert Louis Stevenson challenges, underperformance in learner outcomes is not something to let pass. Great GoaTs do not shy away from the uncomfortable. Instead, they stand before it and stare it down.

PERFORMANCE MANAGEMENT

༄

The next aspect of Performance Management is the Leadership Team, more particularly the Head (or Principal or Chief Executive – we'll stick with Head for now).

The Head's line manager is, of course, the Chief GoaT (aka Chair). While that relationship is pivotal to the smooth running of the organisation, it falls to all GoaTs to hold the Head to account.

What does that mean?

Simply, that the Head is delivering on GoaTs' strategy for the organisation while ensuring that key targets are met.

But the true test of effective performance management is not the doing of it, but the manner in which it is done.

The attributes of great GoaTs are never more in focus as when the leadership of a school or college is under the microscope.

First, they must agree what are the essential measures by which the Head will be judged. These are what, in business-speak, would be seen as mission-critical.

Every school and college will identify these, each according to its specific circumstances.

And if, by some slim chance, that hasn't been done, then it should be on the next board agenda.

Assuming it has, most will be common, even if the numerical targets vary widely.

For example, learner outcomes at relevant Key Stages are indispensable.

As is meeting the annual budget.

There will be a host of other data against which to assess the Head. Most of these will depend on the organisation's past performance, so their ranking of importance (essential vs. desirable) will need to be carefully calibrated.

One example: a sixth-form college with relatively poor attendance will be at risk of reduced funding if students are enrolled but do not attend. Where attendance in a successful peer is never an issue, for this college it could prove existential.

But there will also be softer metrics, at least in terms of the timescale of delivery. The same college that revels in high attendance and retention may well be facing its own challenges in the future if it is unable to grow the roll sufficiently to prevent inflation eroding any year-on-year surplus and, inevitably, its reserves.

So, perhaps, after years of a relatively calm voyage, the prospect of an impending and unavoidable structural deficit focuses the mind, elevating a meaningful strategy to find growth from a 'nice-to-have' to a 'need-to-have'.

Implementing this type of process takes place over years, not months. Performance Management needs milestones en route to enable assessment.

Let's expand this example as an illustration.

In order to grow the roll sufficiently to impact the revenue profile, the options would include a new build, some form of merger or other foundational shift, or investment to grow non-funded revenue.

None of these is achieved in a single year. So GoaTs require clear stages that will need to be met.

'If we build, how do we finance?'

'If we merge, with whom – and why?'

'If we boost income, from where – and how?'

That's how Performance Management rolls out, milestone by milestone, key date by key date. And GoaTs oversee the process, focused on what was said last time, what's being said now – and what they expect to be said next time.

Performance Management of the Head is not just the annual review. It's a continuous process covering the entire role, in all its multifaceted splendour.

೩

And, lastly, there's performance management of the board and its committees, and of individual GoaTs.

Even an Ofsted judgement of Outstanding is no guarantee of continuing excellence. And this is especially true of governance which is not actually inspected; board and committee meetings are not observed by seasoned practitioners, even if minutes are perused.

For that, schools and colleges must turn to an experienced outsider to carry out an external review of governance.

This is the only reliable mechanism to give GoaTs reassurance that the way their board goes about its business accords with recognised high standards.

It serves to shake off any complacency that may embed when things are going well. But it should confirm and complement an annual self-assessment.

A questionnaire that creates the space for self-reflection is a pre-requisite of continuous improvement.

In completing it, GoaTs should be given the opportunity to comment on the performance of both Chair and Clerk.

What's more, they should be able to specify areas of governance where collective and personal improvement would be welcome.

And some boards carry out a regular appraisal of every GoaT, the Chair and Clerk discussing with them individually how they think they're doing, and what they would like to see done differently. This informal process can support continuous improvement of governance, while focusing minds and reinforcing commitment to the cause.

The battle to improve is always waged, but never won.
Robust and forensic performance management is the most indispensable weapon in a GoaT's arsenal. Without it, defeat is inevitable.

Risk

'There are moments when everything goes well; don't be frightened, it won't last.'
Pierre-Jules Renard

Some GoaTs think the glass is half-full.

Others reckon it's half-empty.

The 'never-disappointeds' assume that it's not just half-empty but, when they looked away, someone peed in it.

And that, in a nutshell, encapsulates the varying approaches to risk management across the educational landscape.

Where one institution has an almost zero regard to the risks that may impact the operation, another will have an annual review, while a third will visit the risk register termly.

Which is right?

Well, to some extent, the answer will depend upon the culture of the overarching authority governing the organisation.

In a hands-on LEA, governors (and just them this time) may reasonably expect significant support on some of the principal areas of risk, such as finance, HR and estates.

Others, like performance management and safeguarding, are so 'local' to the school that responsibility for assessing risk rests

THE SCOPE OF GOATSHIP

squarely on the shoulders of leaders and the governing body.

Given that LEAs are responsible for many schools, it falls to individual boards to consider all that might interfere with the smooth running and upward progress of both the school and its learners.

The trustees of MATs will establish the risk culture across the whole trust. Likewise, LEA executive officers should (hopefully) support (or, at least, encourage) governors in community schools to consider and manage the risks most likely to threaten their school.

So, GoaTs must attune their antennae to what can go wrong.

For some, this will be easy. For others, not so much.

But this is not the place to go through all the potential pitfalls. If a GoaT board doesn't have a disciplined risk management process, then one should be demanded.

They are straightforward both to develop and oversee. And will deliver to boards and leadership teams alike the comfort that comes from doing all that can be done to be prepared for the challenging and the unusual.

If the collective view is that any plan is just too granular for oversight by the full board, the answer's simple. Distribute responsibility across the committee structure, utilising, in particular, any audit expertise, as it usually fits well with the disciplines required for effective risk management.

Risk comes in many guises and we're going to look next at one of those areas which can cause most difficulties when GoaTs gather.

Succession Planning

'Out of the crooked timber of humanity no straight thing can ever be made.'
Immanuel Kant

The most important specific task of GoaTs is planning who succeeds the Head and the Chair – and then implementing.

These two roles – and the way their incumbents interact with each other – will be the key factor in how well the organisation is governed and led.

So recruiting to them is of singular significance. Get either wrong and the impact will be both negative and long-lasting.

Bringing in a new Head or replacing a long-standing Chair is fraught with risk. As Kant observed, none of us is perfect – and any selection process is, by its very nature, speculative.

To mitigate the essential danger of this situation requires clear thinking and embedded planning.

The ideal is to avoid surprises. That can't always be the case – but there is a strategic imperative in trying.

Having clear-sighted views of retirement dates and terms of office are essential to effective planning. Any device that can reduce the risk of surprise departures should be deployed.

All Chairs serve fixed terms that can vary from one year to four (with the possibility of extension).

As the relationship with the Head is so pivotal, it is generally desirable to have a longer term than just one year. So, if a school or college's constitution specifies a single year or some such, then GoaTs should have a tacit understanding that, assuming a steady state, there will be an unchallenged re-election at its end.

GoaTs should also be clued in to the ambitions and life plans of the Head.

A long-serving leader is more likely to stay in post until retirement. A younger appointee may well be thinking of new challenges after a while in the job.

The instincts of governance must be alive to the rhythm of the Chair's and Head's contentment in their roles.

For the Head, it falls to the Chair to make sure they understand their hopes and aspirations. While this should take place within the formal annual appraisal, regular and relaxed touching base is also important.

GoaTs should never forget that the Head is most likely to have started their career as a teacher. The dictates of modern educational leadership effectively require them to morph into the chief executive of a multi-million-pound social enterprise.

Not all can do it. And many more don't particularly enjoy it.

Take the example of an experienced deputy head required to be acting head where a succession plan collapsed when the substantive leader resigned one working day before the statutory deadline.

It took half a term for the reality to dawn that he wasn't

SUCCESSION PLANNING

enjoying it, nor could he deliver what the board was demanding in terms of rapidly improved learner outcomes.

Here, GoaTs moved very quickly and defined precisely what kind of Head they needed. The person specification was explicit, ruling out any internal candidates.

Equally decisively, the board decided that the school could afford only one recruitment round.

So, while the campaign unashamedly targeted experienced serving Heads who were looking for their last, career-defining role, an alternative strategy was rolled out in parallel.

The Chair led the search for a multi-academy trust that could take on the school and provide immediate transformational leadership should recruitment fail.

And it worked. An inspirational Head was appointed (and the relationship with at least one MAT was nurtured to maintain options). There's a flowchart of a proven recruitment process on page 102.

All GoaTs should recognise that the cumulative pressures on a Head – results, finance, safeguarding, Ofsted, staff, to name but five –take their toll.

The essence of effective succession planning is to – at the very least – have a strategy to create a strategy. Where a leader is clearly in their last job before retirement, it is reasonable to think about what to do when they eventually step down.

And where there is a sense that this is not their final post, then constructive engagement between Chair and Head may help ensure as smooth a transition as possible, when the time comes for them to move on.

This is as much a question of culture as it is of cold-eyed planning. The goal is clear: ensure that bringing in new people at the top of the organisation enables continuity and a seamless handover.

Succession management, like death and taxes, safeguarding events and Ofsted's arrival, is inevitable.

What's not inevitable is a full-blown crisis.

So, let's look at what happens when one actually hits.

Crisis resolution

'When written in Chinese, the word "crisis" is composed of two characters – one represents danger, and the other opportunity.'
John F Kennedy

First, what actually *is* a crisis? It's a time of immense and immediate difficulty or danger, usually triggered by an event outside the normal operations of a school or college.

That absence of normality means that there will be no policy or embedded practice to guide how to respond. Leaders and GoaTs will be adrift without the lifebelt of experience to keep them afloat.

The initial response will inevitably depend upon the nature of the crisis. But whatever it is, the first reaction must be: Don't panic. Breathe. Take time to think.

If it has been provoked by the leadership itself, then GoaTs – led by the Chair – will need to leap into action.

See, for example, what happened when the two Heads of schools which had merged that very month independently resigned right on the deadline for resignation, leaving no time to find a replacement.

It took just one emergency meeting for governors, first, to vent their frustration (they'd laboured long and hard to develop a post-merger co-headship that both incumbents could sign up to) – and then move on.

Even though the situation was unprecedented, decision-making was swift and decisive. Promote from within, secure external and experienced support, watch progress – and recruit if necessary.

If the crisis is at board level, then it will be almost inevitable that expertise will need to be parachuted in from outside. This may necessitate hands-on involvement from a Regional Director, LEA, ESFA or other agency with oversight and ultimate responsibility for the institution.

Imagine yourself in this situation.

You're a trustee of a single academy trust. There's an implosion of governance. The long-serving Head has been placed on extended absence, following an investigation into a grievance from the departing Deputy Head that found there were issues to be further examined.

The board is divided, split between allies of the Head and the rest. An Ofsted inspection has judged the school 'Requires improvement', but only because of Leadership and Management.

Staff are threatening to strike should the Head return. Parents are petitioning for them to come back. Local media are all over it.

So, what do you do? With the agreement of the Regional Director, the Chair (a reluctant, recent promotion) summoned an outside trouble-shooter to try and bring order to the chaos. At

CRISIS RESOLUTION

the same time, interim executive Heads were sought to support the inexperienced Acting Head who was overwhelmed with her new responsibilities within a fractious and fractured culture.

In circumstances like these, GoaTs (even if they don't actually know it) need leadership. So, it's important that the 'help' makes an immediate impression.

The entire organisation is yearning for calm, for a quiet, authoritative voice that can bring them the comfort they seek: that all will be ok, even if the road ahead will be rocky.

And this is the watchword for all those in the eye of a storm: realism.

GoaTs should demand realism from their external advisers. And they, in their turn, must be blunt in what can be achieved, by when, and what difficulties and sacrifices those achievements will necessitate.

To see how this example panned out, see the flowchart on page 100.

The Chief GoaT

A non-reclining, non-folding Chair

The art of chairing

'A good conductor ought to be a good chauffeur; the qualities that make the one also make the other. They are concentration, an incessant control of attention, and presence of mind.'
Sergei Rachmaninoff

Not for nothing was this section introduced with the phrase 'the art of chairing'.

And not for nothing does it start with a quotation about conducting.

Because the truth is, no two Chief GoaTs are alike. Just like orchestral conductors, they bring their own personality, insight and style to the role, creating something that is unique (even when the score is well known).

And this analogy is particularly apt. An effective Chair treats the board as if it's a small orchestra.

Each instrument has its own voice. It should be heard as such, but must also sound in harmony with the others.

No-one should be louder than the rest; neither do they have the right to play more often than others.

It falls to the Chair to control the distinctive opinions gathered around the table and ensure that all views are considered.

So, what should GoaTs look for when picking a Chair?

Above all else, the key quality is independence – of role, of spirit and of mind.

They don't take sides, but create the space for free and unfettered debate.

They don't ally themselves to the leadership, but retain a distance that allows for a constructive relationship based on trust, mutual respect and clear lines of authority.

They don't assume that the way that's something has been done in the past is the way it must be in the future.

And, most of all, they ensure the board operates independently from the management of the organisation, focusing on its critical job of a deliverable strategy, ever-improving performance and financial sustainability.

This requires them to stand up to other GoaTs if they find walking the bridge between governance and operations too taxing. And it demands that they don't fold should the leadership team prove resistant to GoaT-driven initiatives.

Yet there are other aspects to the role that GoaTs need to bear in mind when thinking about the Chair and how they're doing. Or, indeed, who their successor should be.

Time. Does what they do for a living give them sufficient bandwidth to do the job? Being a Chair is demanding. It's not a job that can be dialled in; neither can it be done well by reclining back rather than leaning forward.

Fostering a healthy and productive relationship with the Head and other leaders requires effort. It needs to be done face-to-face. Some Chairs like to be in school or college weekly. Others less so. Either way, regular contact is essential.

So, for example, the senior partner of a professional firm in a city centre was considering putting his name forward to be the next Chair of an institution on the outskirts, an hour or more's drive from the office.

The annual, predictable workload had to be impressed upon them. This involved breaking down the role description into its component parts alongside itemising the details of how the incumbent actually did the job, much of it out of sight of the rest of the board.

But that's just a blank canvas on which the art of chairing will be created.

Control of effective meetings is the most visible sign of a Chief GoaT's effectiveness.

One of the challenges of selecting a new Chair is that it's quite possible that they have never actually chaired a meeting within the organisation.

So it's a good idea to make sure that chairing is shared around. Committees and working parties provide a great forum to hone the necessary skills. It can prove very constructive to ensure that the Vice Chair takes such a role, particularly if they are potentially a successor to the Chief GoaT.

Strong Chairs are always talent-spotting. They know not to outstay their welcome. Indeed, some institutions have a fixed limit of two four-year terms. The planning should begin at the start of the second of these, with close scrutiny being paid to the colleagues most likely to be able and willing to step up.

Chief GoaTs lead by example. They are constantly trying to

improve while staying on top of the demands of the job.

Curiosity is a useful attribute here. How do other boards in peer institutions operate? Are their Chairs doing things differently, better?

If your Chief GoaT is not mixing with others, comparing notes and challenges, successes and failures, then perhaps they should be.

It's all too easy to function in a silo, hermetically sealed from the sector. No one school or college has a monopoly of wisdom or the most productive of practices.

The notion of a self-improving educational system is rightly hailed as a great idea. But its reach is not restricted to pedagogy or, indeed, any other aspect of the day-to-day functions of a place of learning.

It also stretches to governance and the various networks gathered around this critical function – of Chairs, of Clerks, of GoaTs. They should be ruthlessly exploited to optimise high performance levels by GoaTs across the many diverse types of board.

So, try and build sharing and observation with peers, seeing how meetings are conducted, and how their Chief GoaTs go about the business of chairing.

And, from bitter experience, here's another very personal reason for Chief GoaTs to reach out to their peers and build a community.

I was once on the receiving end of a grievance from a Head. Here's not the place to discuss its merits (or otherwise).

But, from the moment I was informed of it, what was

abundantly clear was how isolated a Chief GoaT actually is.

Whereas a Head is swathed in the armour of employment law, protective policies and trade union membership, a Chair has nothing but their integrity and conscience.

It's then that the investment you've made in supporting other Chief GoaTs and being a good (if somewhat critical) friend begins to repay itself.

It certainly proved its value to me in what was a truly difficult time.

The Tribe of GoaTs

Attributes of an effective board

Hallmarks of Excellence

'A tribe is a group of people connected to one another, connected to a leader, and connected to an idea.'
Seth Godin

'Tribe' is a great word for a gathering of GoaTs. (As it happens, it's also one of the four recognised collective nouns for the actual bovid, along with 'flock', 'trips' and 'tripe'.)

Indeed, you might say that while goats are ruminants, GoaTs ruminate.

Effective boards are thoughtful. They reflect on what they're told. And they ask penetrating and relevant questions.

Individual GoaTs are connected to one another by the concept of public service, amplified through the noble filter of volunteering. Led by the Chair, their connecting idea is that by investing their individual experience, insights and know-how, they can help create successful schools and colleges that are sustainably stable.

Some boards sign up to a charter or code of conduct in order to embed shared values. You can find an example on page 99.

But they can only succeed if the forums where they connect are professional, transparent and forensic.

And that can only happen if meetings happen under certain key conditions.

So, let's take a look at the features of effective GoaT gatherings through the prism of those three cornerstones of effective governance: Preparation, Attendance, Participation.

What is 'preparation'? It's where GoaTs immerse themselves in all information germane to a meeting thanks to the timely provision of accessible and comprehensive information, where:

'timely provision' = making available papers sufficiently in advance of a meeting to allow for careful reading;

'accessible' = papers created in a way that allows for ease of comprehension (with complexity, jargon and extraneous data stripped out), alongside explanatory notes, where necessary, to ensure lay GoaTs are able to prepare properly;

'comprehensive' = a complete explanation of the particular topic or issue, ideally with a balanced, objective position set out by the author, rather than a subjective argument that emphasises only one side of the matter.

And what of 'attendance'? Well, that's rather more straightforward.

It means regularly making meetings, whether in person or remotely.

A GoaT who frequently misses meetings is, quite simply, not a GoaT. They are a CV stuffer or, perhaps, a compulsive gatherer of positions and titles, albeit possibly well-meaning.

Strong boards take pride in stellar attendance stats. And they begrudge any colleague who serially undermines those data.

So Chief GoaTs have to step up and sort this out – quickly. It

HALLMARKS OF EXCELLENCE

weakens team spirit and can sow seeds of discontent.

The only pathway is to apply the rules relating to absence rigorously – and remove the non-GoaT as quickly as possible.

Which leaves 'participation'.

There is a difference between attending a meeting and participating in it.

Participation is active, not passive. It involves, no, *demands*, engagement in every item on the agenda.

This is, of course, made possible by diligent preparation. Going through the supporting documentation, marking it up, asking questions, ensuring that it's all understood.

For newer GoaTs, this process can be accelerated by buddying up with an experienced colleague, one who can explain the background to issues, shortcut the history, or explain processes and procedures.

It can be both helpful and reassuring to have someone to contact before meetings or sit beside during them for guidance and advice.

Participation is one of those features easier to recognise than define precisely.

Participative meetings are characterised by anyone who wishes to contribute being able to do so.

It is where GoaTs bide their time before they are called, rather than interrupting and cutting across those who are speaking or waiting to do so.

It is the Chair constantly looking around to see who wants to make a point.

It is GoaTs asking informed questions that have not already

been answered in the pre-meeting pack.

And it is where papers previously circulated are not repeated verbatim, but summarised and, where necessary, updated. They are assumed to have been digested and understood.

On the other side of the coin, what are the enemies of participation?

Tedious and repetitious read-outs of papers, rather than summaries.

Advocacy of positions and issues, rather than the setting out of objectives and balanced pros and cons.

The odd, sometimes very odd, GoaT holding forth on some pet project or other hobbyhorse.

Poorly argued papers that haven't been prepared with the audience in mind. Authors can forget that the impact of messages is not how they leave, but how they arrive.

Proposals which lack a business case frequently trigger extended deliberations that invariably end up with rejection and a resubmission to the next meeting. This can be particularly frustrating for leaders when the issue is time-critical – but that is never a justification for bad decision-making.

All these negatives can suck the life out of meetings and make them far more of a chore than they should be.

If gatherings of GoaTs are not rich and rewarding, then the role does not give back to volunteers all that it should.

And, yes, humour has its place. In fact, it is not too much of a stretch to say that if GoaTs aren't laughing then they're insufficiently engaged.

Repartee is one of the key signs of a healthy board. Meetings that proceed in a dull and procedural fashion will neither inspire nor build team spirit.

Sure, some matters are deadly serious. No-one who has attended (often emergency) meetings dealing with a major safeguarding issue or an existential crisis will deny the tension that hangs heavily in the air.

But, even then, a spark of humour can release the pressure and, if not leaven the matter itself, at least lighten the mood.

This is not to suggest that a Chair or other GoaT prepares a set of jokes. Rather, it is about creating a culture where anyone can chip in with a witty remark, if they think it's appropriate.

They are rarely funny when recounted later but, at the time, such wisecracks can be a welcome relief.

And if you want one symbol of effective boards, look no further than the paper trail from agenda through minutes to actions and decisions.

Are those actions and decisions followed up at the next meeting?

Are GoaTs on top of what needed to be progressed and do they follow up on promises made by leaders on any given issue?

And are they held to account for their failure to deliver on those promises?

All of which brings us to the one indispensable element of great governance …

The Clerk

'I do not rule Russia: ten thousand clerks do.'
Tsar Nicholas II

There can never be great governance if the board is not supported by an independent and professional clerk.

'Professional' here does not merely mean one who is paid.

It refers rather to the way they go about their job.

They don't allow the school or college to deliver papers too close to a meeting.

They remind leaders of the actions arising from the previous meeting to ensure that progress has been made or objectives achieved.

Even while taking minutes, another part of their brain is checking that procedure is being properly applied.

And they are ready to advise the Chair on any aspect of proper governance and efficient meeting management.

Strong clerks produce accurate and comprehensive minutes to a timescale that allows for effective recall and speedy correction. As a guide, this would be something along the lines of 48–72 hours turnround of a draft to the meeting's Chair and the school or college leader.

This allows for checks and corrections before sharing with the group who attended, hopefully within a further 48–72 hours.

One of the key attributes of a great clerk is an insatiable appetite for self-improvement. That manifests itself both in improving skills, and in maintaining mastery of the mass of regulation, guidance and advice that pours out from government and other regulatory and membership bodies.

Only when GoaTs confront this large – and growing – body of rules and oversight can they fully appreciate how pivotal is the role of their clerk in ensuring both comprehension and compliance.

Let's just remind ourselves of these myriad sources.

The Academies Minister, Ofsted, Regional Director and the Education and Skills Funding Agency are all looking from the outside in.

And within the school or college itself will be a raft of constitutional provisions to be complied with or otherwise navigated:

Articles of Association

Instrument and Articles of Government (for those sixth form colleges yet to academise)

Scheme of Delegation

Funding agreement

Academy trust handbook

Department for Education governance guides

LEAs' own governance protocols, and

Each institution's own rule book, evolved over many years of governance and, no doubt, of varying standards and questionable relevance.

And then there's all the training and other support that comes from organisations like the National Governance Association.

The best clerks are on top of all this, gently herding their GoaTs towards excellence.

If your board has such a one, then show them how much they are valued and valuable.

And, if you don't, see how they can be raised up to these standards – or how the absent skills can alternatively be sourced.

A Particular Breed of GoaT

The special case of Trust Members

Members: the Overseers' Overseers

'But who will guard the guards themselves?'
Juvenal

Even the most ardent advocate of the academy system would acknowledge that the role of Trust Member has lacked definition.

When the Blair government launched academies, it adopted the charity governance model.

This meant that – unlike, say, the constitution of sixth form colleges – the full rigour of company law would apply to academies and their emergent cousins, free schools.

One peculiar aspect of this would be that the entity operating the schools would be a company limited by guarantee.

To provide that guarantee, a new level of governance and a different kind of governance beast would be needed.

Welcome to the world of Trust Members.

It is important to aim for distance between the members and the board of trustees. There is a risk of cosiness between the two forums, and the perennial debate on whether the Chair of Trustees ought also to be a member has not yet been satisfactorily resolved.

There can be a tendency to source members from retiring trustees. This does not always hold the promise of objectivity which is essential when the core purpose of members is borne in mind.

There are two descriptors of the key elements of Member oversight:

'Guardians of Governance', and

'Keepers of the Flame'.

So, what do these look like?

A guardian of governance makes sure that the trustees are doing their job.

This means that they are setting the strategy, and ensuring that it is achieving its milestones and end-objectives.

It also means that they are managing performance, while ensuring financial stability.

Members tend to meet at most twice a year, once at the end of the academic year, and in December to receive the annual report and accounts.

This is not theirs to approve. When they get it, it has already been signed off by auditors and the board of trustees.

No, it is theirs to use as the key tool in assessing trustee performance.

Members should pore over the document, identifying areas where they should interrogate the response of trustees to specific issues.

This could be underperformance at particular Key Stages, or concerning financial trends.

Equally, though, it may be high turnover among trustees or unacceptably low attendance by specific individuals.

But it might also be a number of mistakes that suggests

a lack of forensic attention to detail among the leaders of the organisation.

And what of 'keepers of the flame'?

Every trust has a mission, a reason to exist. Members hold trustees to account that the mission is being adhered to.

It's not set in stone. But it should always be the North Star by which trustees steer the trust.

For example, let's say government policy decrees that no MAT should have fewer than 7,500 learners (which recently was the actual case).

A trust that had set its mission as being home to half that number would clearly have to recalibrate. Failure to do so could result in the Keepers of the Flame seeking explanations for any proposed expansion of the trust.

So it is reasonable for members to be included in headline strategic debates (but not decision-making). This is particularly important when it is driven by trustees and leadership thinking that the current mission needs a revamp (or, indeed, wholesale reinvention).

Overall, the key role for members is to ensure that trustees know that their performance will be scrutinised.

The cold, hard fact is that Ofsted purports to report on governance but doesn't ever include governance professionals on an inspection team.

And, as has already been said, while they would never judge the effectiveness of teaching without observing a lesson, such rigour does not extend to governance.

There are several ways members can have comfort that the

MEMBERS: THE OVERSEERS' OVERSEERS

actual proceedings of trustees are effective and compliant.

Most reassuring is a regular external review of governance. Done properly, it will include the observation of a board (and, hopefully, committee) meeting.

The expert in governance carrying it out will also review papers, minutes and outcomes, and ensure they are followed through.

Members should read the ensuing report carefully and critically. They ought to include in their own agenda how recommendations have been implemented and suggestions followed up.

The exercise should be repeated every three years or so, particularly if the last report was critical, there has been significant churn in trustee numbers, or the Chief GoaT has moved on.

But there is also an argument that members themselves should observe board meetings or, at least, read minutes.

This should deliver reassurance to all members that they are 'on the case', while also beefing up the role beyond just two meetings a year.

And, when they do meet, members should feel free to ask of any issue in which they are interested: Have trustees taken a position on this? What was it? How did they assure themselves that the leadership was across it? Have they monitored progress? What degree of challenge did the trust board exert?

All this can make the job simpler to explain and more attractive and engaged, thus easing recruitment to a stratum of governance that can be challenging to fill.

Nolan

The seven principles of public life

Best Behaviour

'Behaviour is a mirror in which everyone displays his own image.'
Johann Wolfgang von Goethe

For GoaTs seeking guidance on their own behaviour (or that of their colleagues), the Seven Principles of Public Life ('Nolan Principles') are *the* place to start.

It's worth keeping them both in mind and to hand, particularly if there is concern about how fellow GoaTs (or even the Chief GoaT) are conducting themselves.

SELFLESSNESS
Holders of public office should act solely in terms of the public interest.

INTEGRITY
Holders of public office must avoid placing themselves under any obligation to people or organisations that might try inappropriately to influence them in their work. They should not act or take decisions in order to gain financial or other material benefits for themselves, their family or their friends. They must declare and resolve any interests and relationships.

OBJECTIVITY
Holders of public office must act and take decisions impartially, fairly and on merit, using the best evidence and without discrimination or bias.

ACCOUNTABILITY
Holders of public office are accountable to the public for their decisions and actions and must submit themselves to the scrutiny necessary to ensure this.

OPENNESS
Holders of public office should act and take decisions in an open and transparent manner. Information should not be withheld from the public unless there are clear and lawful reasons for so doing.

HONESTY
Holders of public office should be truthful.

LEADERSHIP
Holders of public office should exhibit these principles in their own behaviour and treat others with respect. They should actively promote and robustly support the principles and challenge poor behaviour wherever it occurs.

A Stimulus to Challenge

Some suggestions for how to start the conversation

No-Conflict Questions

'Ask an impertinent question, and you are on the way to a pertinent answer.'
Jacob Bronowski

For many GoaTs, particularly those who are new to the role, asking challenging questions can be daunting. Some are even cowed into perpetual silence.

But it doesn't have to be like that. As experience grows – and the example of colleagues exerts itself – each GoaT should develop their own style and technique for getting the information they seek.

So, here's a brief list of some of the questions that can be posed without implied criticism or otherwise appearing confrontational.

They work (probably with some tweaking) in a number of situations, including reviewing business proposals or other innovations, as well as when results of external inspections, tests and examinations are reviewed.

What does success look like?

NO-CONFLICT QUESTIONS

What are the barriers to success?

☙

How did we achieve that success?

☙

... and what needs to be done to repeat it?

☙

Is there anything we could have done differently?

☙

What can we learn from major peers?

☙

What have we not *thought of?*

☙

What if we don't *do it?*

☙

Have you done a risk assessment?

☙

Does doing this address anything identified in our SWOT?

And, finally, Exiting your GoaTship

What to do when disappointment hits

Avoiding the Dread

'The fundamental cause of the trouble is that in the modern world the stupid are cocksure while the intelligent are full of doubt.'
Bertrand Russell

Let's be honest. Not every GoaTship will work out.

Some find the job too onerous, particularly in and around meetings.

Others just can't make the schedule work around the rest of their life.

There will be those who just find it all too tedious and can't make the contribution they hoped for.

Then, there will be colleagues whose beliefs or behaviour make the atmosphere around the table too unpleasant (or toxic) to make GoaTship the rich and rewarding experience it should be.

Despite Bertrand Russell, it doesn't follow that all those who ooze confidence are stupid, or that colleagues who are uncertain are intelligent.

But it does follow that there will be alpha GoaTs who are both boring and boorish, with a tendency to mount their hobbyhorses before riding them to exhaustion.

AND, FINALLY, EXITING YOUR GOATSHIP

In any of these circumstances (and many more besides), the key to contentment is transparency.

Talk to the Chair and the Clerk and explain your reservations. Don't be like that GoaT who, after four years on the Finance Committee, explained at his final meeting that he'd never understood a word of it.

Stand up and show that you have doubts. There's no shame or weakness in it. On the contrary, it reveals a strength of character and self-knowledge that are truly powerful.

It could be that some extra training would be beneficial. Perhaps, some mentoring or a more proactive buddy could increase confidence.

And it is almost certain that the irritating alpha is annoying more people than just you.

If there's no solution, then step away gracefully and look for another way to put your social conscience to work.

Being a GoaT should be one of the best things in your life.

If the way you earn your money lacks something meaningful, then serving on the board of a school or college can give you work:work balance.

You can see what contribution you're making, regardless of whether the organisation is securely stable, or in need of strategic realignment or crisis resolution.

Sure, there will be times when, even in the best ordered institution, something hits that is totally unexpected.

It could be a major safeguarding incident. Or a controversial exclusion. Perhaps, a sudden dip in outcomes. Maybe, a surprise hole opens up in the finances.

All of these can, in some way, be prepared for through risk management, and clear policies and procedures.

But it's the collective response from GoaTs that will, to a considerable extent, determine success.

And when it happens – and it *will* happen – you'll look back with some satisfaction that when you were called upon to be great, you were equal to the challenge.

You won't necessarily be remembered for it. Generations of learners passing through the classrooms won't even know your name.

But *you* will know. Executed with diligence and integrity, GoaTship has the potential for impact and legacy long into the future.

And you will have the warm glow of a job well done, amplified through the nobility of volunteering.

It's one of the golden threads that run through the life of great GoaTs.

Relish it.

Some Case Studies and Tools

Here are just a few tools that may help GoaTs be even greater.
You're welcome to request full-size copies by emailing
ian@cleweducation.uk

Governance charter model

SCHOOL GOVERNANCE CHARTER

MISSION OF THE GOVERNING BODY

Our mission is to ensure that our school has clarity of vision, a strong, well-understood ethos, and a clear strategic direction.

❦

It is the role of governors to hold the Head to account for learner outcomes, the management of staff performance, and how well the school spends public money.

VALUES OF THE GOVERNING BODY

We will conduct business through three distinct behaviours: scrutinising performance, challenging plans and actions, supporting the School leadership.

❦

Individual opinions are freely expressed but decisions are collective and binding.

❦

Confidentiality is an absolute standard of our proceedings and no governor will share information without permission.

❦

Our loyalty is to the school and not to individual governors or leaders.

❦

Preparation, attendance and participation are the benchmarks of governors' effectiveness.

❦

Documents submitted to, or emanating from, the Governing Body will strive to be models of clarity and transparency.

Agreed by the Governing Body: date

SOME CASE STUDIES AND TOOLS

Academy crisis resolution case study

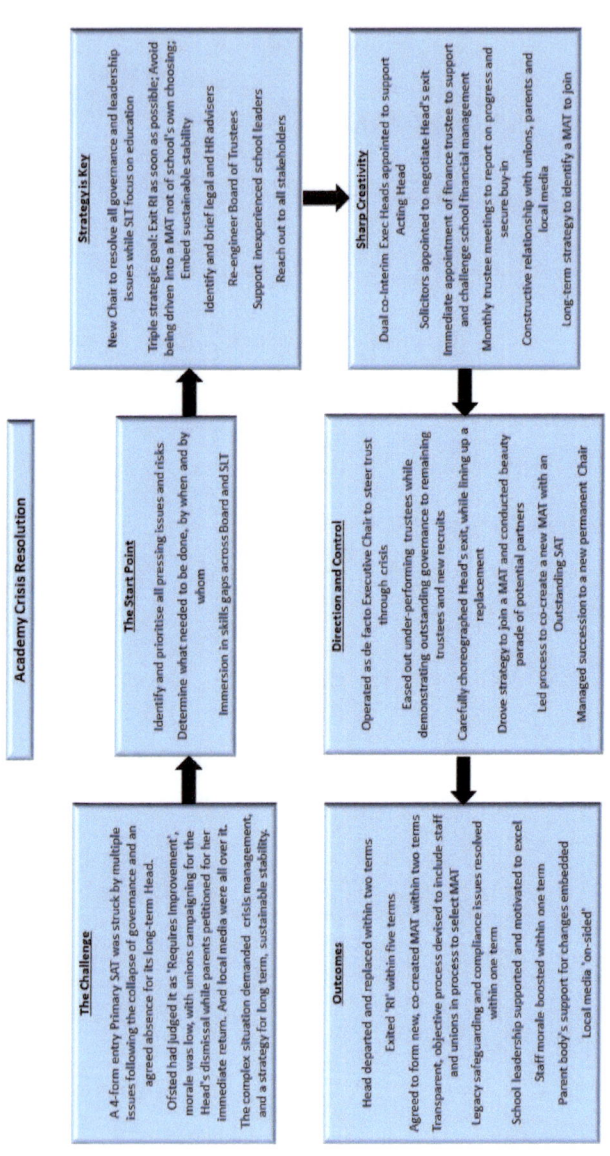

School transformation case study

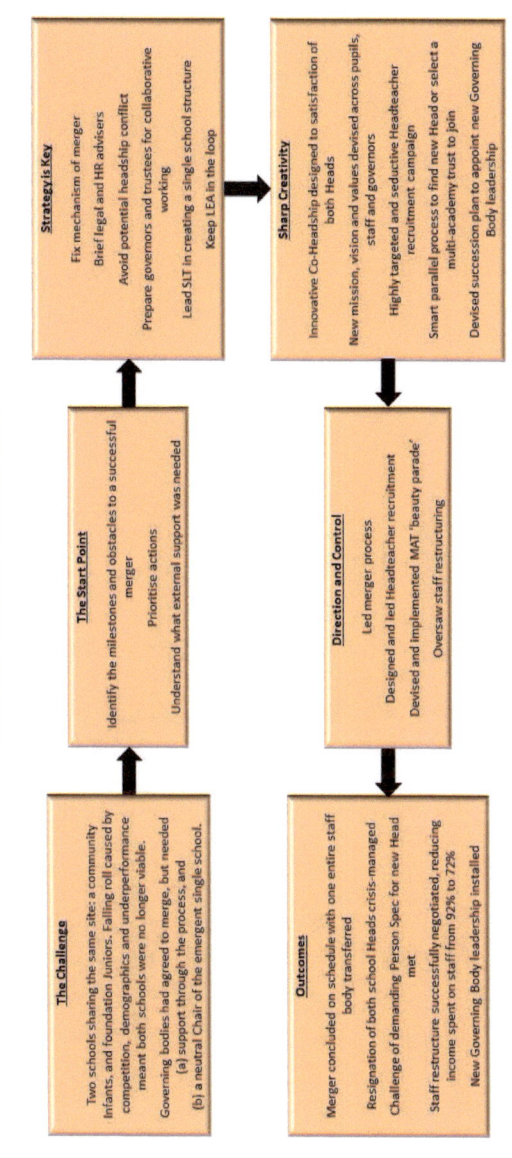

School Transformation

The Challenge
Two schools sharing the same site: a community Infants, and foundation Juniors. Falling roll caused by competition, demographics and underperformance meant both schools were no longer viable. Governing bodies had agreed to merge, but needed (a) support through the process, and (b) a neutral Chair of the emergent single school.

The Start Point
Identify the milestones and obstacles to a successful merger
Prioritise actions
Understand what external support was needed

Strategy is Key
Fix mechanism of merger
Brief legal and HR advisers
Avoid potential headship conflict
Prepare governors and trustees for collaborative working
Lead SLT in creating a single school structure
Keep LEA in the loop

Sharp Creativity
Innovative Co-Headship designed to satisfaction of both Heads
New mission, vision and values devised across pupils, staff and governors
Highly targeted and seductive Headteacher recruitment campaign
Smart parallel process to find new Head or select a multi-academy trust to join
Devised succession plan to appoint new Governing Body leadership

Direction and Control
Led merger process
Designed and led Headteacher recruitment
Devised and implemented MAT 'beauty parade'
Oversaw staff restructuring

Outcomes
Merger concluded on schedule with one entire staff body transferred
Resignation of both school Heads crisis-managed
Challenge of demanding Person Spec for new Head met
Staff restructure successfully negotiated, reducing income spent on staff from 92% to 72%
New Governing Body leadership installed

SOME CASE STUDIES AND TOOLS

Leader recruitment flowchart

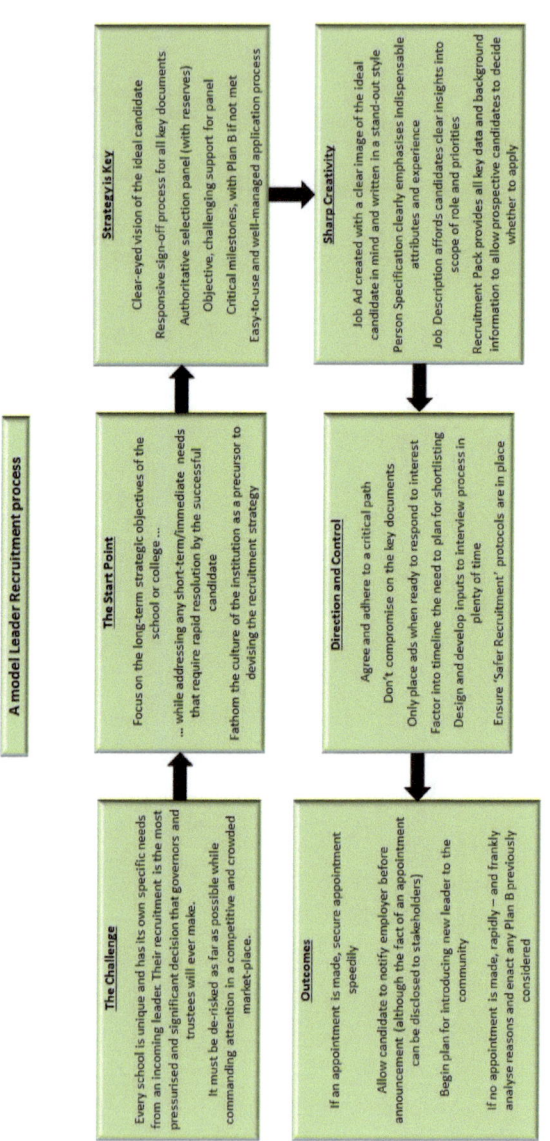

Skills audit + board profile model

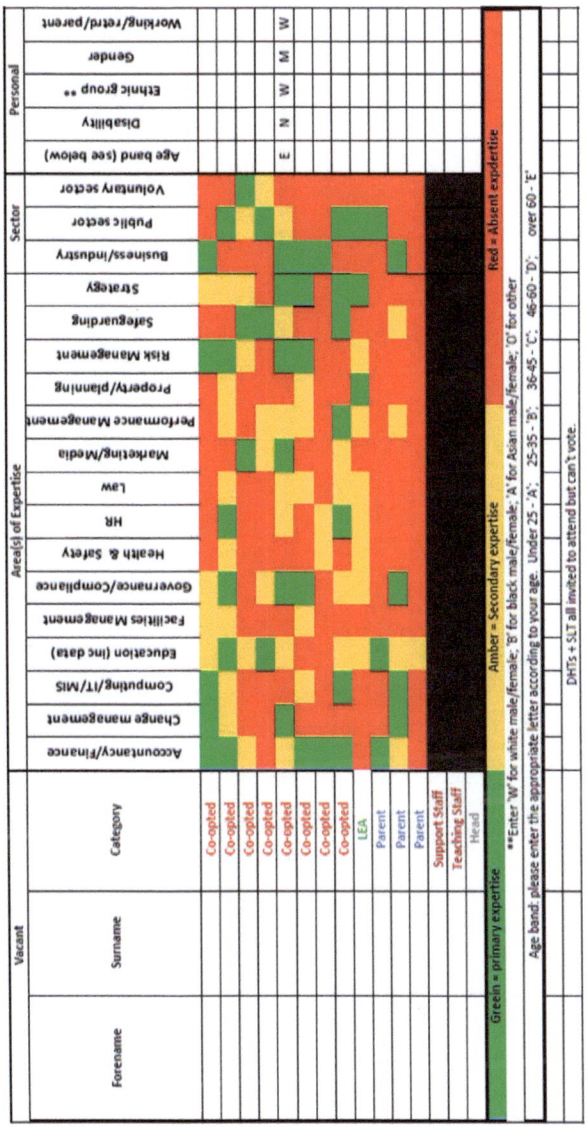

SOME CASE STUDIES AND TOOLS

Model Pros & Cons 1-pager

This page provides the basis of a balanced consultation with staff to advance understanding of the choices facing the school in terms of whether to commit to the MAT now – or wait.

In April, trustees agreed it to be in the long-term interests of stakeholders (pupils, staff, parents, DfE, ESFA, and Regional Director) that the school joins a MAT. The overarching strategic driver is to build sustainable stability so that all stakeholders can take comfort from the fact that the school has secure foundations and it can do what it does best: teach children.

MODEL PROS AND CONS: MAT MEMBERSHIP

It formed this view based on two clear facts: one, we are already a single academy trust; and, two, it is 'RI'. Trustees also bore in mind: their understanding of the root causes of the school's issues, a collective reading of the political runes with their direction of travel towards MATs, and a belief that only SATs that are sustainably outstanding could resist enforced entry into a MAT.

In expressing a preference for the chosen MAT, trustees took account of responses to criteria and questions, alongside meetings with the leaders of three MATs.

Trustees recognise and welcome the staff voice as a critical part of the decision-making process, and wish to engage proactively openly and transparently. Everyone needs to be clear about what it means to join the MAT, or to stay as we are.

The bullets are not prioritised in any way, and colleagues are invited to add, remove and amend, as well as apply their own criteria to determine which are more important, and which are less.

OPTION	PRO	CON
Join MAT now	<ul><li>The ability to retain the school's identity</li><li>Known, strong, benign leadership</li><li>Knows our school, warts and all</li><li>Clear through-age strategy</li><li>Strong leadership cohort</li><li>Definite local solution with new 'neutral' brand</li><li>Able to shape the model, leadership, strategy & culture</li><li>Immediate injection of strategic trustee & SLT skills</li><li>Career progression opportunities</li><li>Formal engagement with a sustainably outstanding school</li></ul>	<ul><li>Nascent MAT, so no experience</li><li>Still to strengthen Board in readiness for MAT</li><li>Unknown factor in terms of leadership</li><li>Might it be 'betting the farm' too early?</li><li>Could it reduce staff morale post-HMI?</li><li>Potential for job losses</li><li>Loss of some independence/autonomy/identity</li><li>No longer totally self-sufficient</li></ul>
Wait	<ul><li>More choices later</li><li>New opportunities may emerge</li><li>Post-RI would be in strong position to lead MAT</li><li>'Cultural revolution' embeds excellence everywhere</li><li>More likely to be able to lead/shape MAT</li><li>A mature MAT should still want us</li><li>New government may lead to change of policies</li><li>Reaction against MATs stimulates policy review</li></ul>	<ul><li>Risk of being forced into MAT not of our choosing</li><li>Local landscape shifts, leaving us behind</li><li>Less control of our destiny, as academisation pace hots up</li><li>MAT will have built its infrastructure so career opportunities may be more scarce</li><li>Impact and workload of 'cultural revolution', including audit of Board/SLT skills needed to run SAT on business-as-usual basis and embed excellence</li></ul>

104

Model Project Investment Proposal

PROJECT INVESTMENT PROPOSAL FOR BOARD/COMMITTEE CONSIDERATION

Project Name			
Project Description			
Input received to date from (e.g. professional advisers/board members)			
Total Project Costs (Confirmed or Estimated?)	One-off		Annually Recurring
	£		£
Less external funding (grants, rentals, etc.)	£		£
Net Cost	£		£
Description of benefits			
Financial Benefits (e.g. additional learners, income, lower costs, or avoided costs)			
Financial Indicators (e.g. payback period or net present value)			
Effect on other projects, if any.			
Impact on Cash Position			
Timings [e.g. approvals needed (Board, Funders, Planners), tenders, build time, etc.]			
Presented by		Date	

About the Author

Ian Phillips was a freelance strategic writer before formalising his governance experience into a commercial offer at www.cleweducation.uk.

He has been involved in governance since 2002. Here's his history.

ABOUT THE AUTHOR

2002–2018	Woodhouse College (**Parent Governor**, then **Chair of Governors** for 12 years)
2007–2010	UK Government FE Communications Gateway Practitioner Panel (**Member**)
2014–2016	Sixth Form Colleges Association (**National Council – London Governor Representative, London SFC Chairs' Forum convener**)
2014–2020	National College for Teaching & Leadership etc. (**National Leader of Governance**), various training and review assignments, leading to …
2016–now	Sudbury Primary School (**Chair of Trustees** and **Members**), crisis resolution, then co-created Chrysalis Multi Academy Trust (**Trust Member**)
2018	SFCA (**Annual Governance award**)
2018–2019	Focus Fitness UK (**Founding Chair, Governance Supervisory Board**)
2018–2021	Dollis Infants and Junior Schools (**Consultant/Project Manager, amalgamation**), then Dollis Primary School (**Chair**)
2019–now	Westfield Academy Trust (**Trust Member**)
2020–now	Frontier Learning Trust (**Trust Member**) – new MAT for Woodhouse College & Imperial College London Maths School
2021–now	Grasvenor Avenue Infant School Academy Trust (**Chair of Trustees** – overseeing closure)
2022–2023	Squires Lane Learning Federation (**Chair of Governors**)
2023–now	Watling Park School (**Chair, Local Advisory Board**, within Bellevue Place Education Trust)
2023–now	Garden Suburb Schools (**Governor**)

About the Sponsor

Bellevue Place Education Trust

ABOUT THE SPONSOR

Bellevue Place Education Trust (BPET) is a multi-academy trust which supports a growing number of schools across London and Berkshire.

Its vision is to deliver the highest standards of education, blended from the best of the state and independent sectors. BPET aims for all children it serves to Learn, Enjoy, Succeed.

All its schools have been judged by Ofsted to be Good, Good with Outstanding features, with four Outstanding. Pupil achievement is high, with pupil on average achieving 10 per cent above national average, driven by a broad and balanced curriculum delivered across all schools.

BPET is an educational charity that is proud to offer an exciting model of education, using the experiences of the independent schools sector, combined with the efficiency of a private sector company, and offer this to all children via state schools.

If your school or college would welcome an informal chat about life in a MAT, BPET's CEO, Mark Greatrex can be reached at info@bpet.co.uk.

https://www.bpet.co.uk/

Notes